LIFE CYCLES

POLAR LANDS

Sean Callery
Consultant: David Burnie

KINGFISHER

First published 2011 by Kingfisher
This edition published 2018 by Kingfisher
an imprint of Macmillan Children's Books
20 New Wharf Road, London N1 9RR
Associated companies throughout the world
www.panmacmillan.com

ISBN 978-0-7534-4282-1

Printed in China
9 8 7 6 5 4 3 2 1
1TR/0917/WKT/UNTD/128MA

A CIP catalogue record for this book is available from the British Library.

Note to readers: the website addresses listed in this book are correct at the time of going to print.
However, due to the ever-changing nature of the internet, website addresses and content can change.
Websites can contain links that are unsuitable for children. The publisher cannot be held
responsible for changes in website addresses or content, or for information obtained through
a third party. We strongly advise that internet searches be supervised by an adult.

The publisher would like to thank the following for permission to reproduce their material. Every care has been taken to trace copyright holders.
top = t; bottom = b; centre = c; left = l; right = r

All artwork Stuart Jackson-Carter (Peter Kavanagh Art Agency)

Cover all images iStock; page 1 Shutterstock/AndreAnita; 2 Shutterstock/Volodymyr Golnyk; 3tl Shutterstock/Miroslav Hlavka; 3br Shutterstock/Sylvie Bouchard; 4t Shutterstock/
TTphoto; 4b Alamy/Mike Cavaroc; 5t Frank Lane Picture Agency (FLPA)/Jim Brandenburg/Minden; 5b Shutterstock/Thomas Barrat; 6bl Alamy/FLPA; 7tl Naturepl/Jane Burton;
7tr Shutterstock/Dmitry Maslov; 7ct FLPA/Gerard Lacz; 7c Alamy/blickwinkel; 7cb Shutterstock/Jo-K; 7cr Shutterstock/Oleg Fokin; 7b Shutterstock/Sergey Uryadnikov;
7br Shutterstock/blinow61; 8bl FLPA/Jasper Doest/Foto Natura; 8tr FLPA/Dickie Duckett; 8br Naturepl/Steve Knell; 9tl FLPA/Danny Ellinger/Foto Natura; 9tr Shutterstock/
Witold Kaszkin; 9ct FLPA/Malcolm Schuyl; 9c Shutterstock/Sergey Uryadnikov; 9cb FLPA/Malcolm Schuyl; 9cr Shutterstock/Gail Johnson; 9br Shutterstock/nialat; 9bl iStock/
VictorTyakht; 10bl Shutterstock/Sam Chadwick; 10tr Ardea/Rolfe Kopfle; 10br Photoshot/NHPA; 11tl Ardea/M. Watson; 11tc Shutterstock/Arto Hakola; 11tr Shutterstock/
Sergey Uryadnikov; 11ct Naturepl/T. J. Rich; 11c Naturepl/Steven Kazlowski; 11cb Shutterstock/nialat; 11cr Shutterstock/Volodymyr Golnyk; 11br Shutterstock/FloridaStock;
11bl Naturepl/Steven Kazlowski; 12bl iStock/USO; 12tr Alamy/John Schwieder; 12br Alamy/Steve Bloom; 13tl Alamy/RGB Ventures/Superstock; 13tr Shutterstock/Gail
Johnson; 13ct Shutterstock/Heather M Davidson; 13c Naturepl/Steven Kazlowski; 13cb Naturepl/Andy Rouse; 13cr Shutterstock/Susannah Grant; 13br Shutterstock/FloridaStock;
13bl Naturepl/T. J. Rich; 14bl Image Quest Marine; 15tl FLPA/Flip Nicklin; 15ct FLPA/Flip Nicklin; 15c Image Quest Marine; 15cb Image Quest Marine; 15cr Shutterstock/
Catamando; 15br Alamy/Niels Poulsen DK; 15b Shutterstock/Andrea Zabiello; 17tr Shutterstock/Gen Productions; 17br Shutterstock/Mogens Trolle; 18bl Corbis/Tim Davis;
18tr Alamy/Johner Images; 18br iStock/karenfoleyphotography; 19tl Alamy/age fotostock; 19tr Shutterstock/Netfalls; 19ct Shutterstock/Leksele; 19c Corbis/DLILLC; 19cb iStock/
Keith Szafranski; 19cr Shutterstock/Alexander Potapov; 19br Shutterstock/jaggcc; 19b Shutterstock/Alexander Potapov; 19bl Alamy/blickwinkel; 20bl Naturepl/Carol Walker;
20tr Alamy/David Chapman; 21tl FLPA/Otto Plantema/Foto Natura; 21tr Shutterstock/Vladimir Melnik; 21ct Shutterstock/Mogens Trolle; 21c Corbis/Frans Lemmens;
21cb Alamy/NielsPoulsen DK; 21cr Shutterstock/Vladimir Melnik; 21b Shutterstock/toomasill; 21b Shutterstock/Vladimir Melnik; 21bl FLPA/Sunset; 22bl Seapics/Dan Burton;
22tr Getty/ Burt Curtsinger/NGS; 22br Getty/Burt Curtsinger/NGS; 23tl Alamy/A&J Visage; 23tr Shutterstock/DPS; 23ct Image Quest Marine; 23c Image Quest Marine;
23cb Getty/Frank Greenaway/DK; 23cr Image Quest Marine; 23br Shutterstock/Rich Carey; 23bl Photoshot/NHPA/Trevor McDonald; 24bl Getty/Paul Nicklin; 24br Getty/Thorsten
Milse; 25ct iStock/Leppakiver; 25c Alamy/Todd Mintz; 25cb Getty/Paul Nicklin; 25bc Shutterstock/Madlen; 25cr Shutterstock/Birute Vljekiene; 25br Shutterstock/Denis Pepin;
25bc Shutterstock/Ricardo Esplana Babor; 25bl Alamy/RGB Ventures; 26bl FLPA/Jim Brandenberg/Minden; 26tr iStock/bjmc; 26br FLPA/Jim Brandenberg/Minden; 27tl Alamy/
Prisma by Dukas Pressagentur GmbH; 27tr Shutterstock/Dim154; 27ct Shutterstock/Christian Musat; 27c Shutterstock/Bianka Berankova; 27cb Getty/Raimund Linke;
27br Alamy/Charles Williams; 27b Shutterstock/Volodymyr Davydenko; 27bl FLPA/Jim Brandenberg/Minden; 30tl Shutterstock/Armin Rose; 30br Shutterstock/Gentoo
Multimedia Ltd.; 31tr Shutterstock/Gentoo Multimedia Ltd.; 31bc Shutterstock/Gentoo Multimedia Ltd. 32l Shutterstock/Jan Martin Will; 32r Shutterstock/Leksele

Contents

Introduction

The Arctic and the Antarctic regions are known as the polar lands. These are the toughest habitats in the world: dark all winter long, with freezing temperatures and storms. Against the odds, plants and animals live here.

Food chain 1

ARCTIC

Arctic ocean

Food chain 3

Most food chains start with living things that make their own food using the sun's energy. They are known as producers and include algae, lichens, mosses and grasses.

SOUTH AMERICA

All living things have to eat to stay alive. Some make their own food using the sun's energy, some eat plants and many try to eat each other. The list of who eats who is called a food chain.

The first animal in a food chain is called a primary consumer because it eats other living things. A moose, for example, eats grasses and moss in the Arctic.

Food chain 2

Next in a food chain is what is known as a secondary consumer. It eats smaller, slower prey. An Arctic fox, for example, eats lemmings, hares, birds and their eggs.

This book takes you along two food chains from the Arctic and one from the Antarctic. You will find out about the life cycles of 11 animals: how they are born, grow, reproduce and die.

Equator

AFRICA

At the end of a food chain is a top predator like a polar bear. It is too big and strong for other animals to attack, and it eats huge numbers of seals, fish and other animals.

AUSTRALIA

Southern ocean

ANTARCTICA

Hermit crab

Hairy hermit crabs are scavengers that eat dead plants and animals which would otherwise rot. In this way, they help to keep the Arctic sea and shore clean. They live in the shells of dead sea animals.

1 The female carries thousands of eggs inside her shell. When they grow big enough, she releases them. Each egg hatches into a larva when it reaches the water outside.

2 As the larva grows claws and feelers, it sheds its outer shell, the exoskeleton, and grows a larger one. This process is called moulting.

4 When it becomes an adult, the crab finds an empty shell to live in. It outgrows its shell again and again throughout its life. Each time, it must pull itself out of the old shell and run to a new home.

3 The larva moults several times. It burrows into the sand while it grows a new exoskeleton, which takes ten days to harden. Each time it moults, the larva looks more like an adult crab.

Did you know?

The hermit crab uses its claws for fighting, grabbing food and picking up its next shell. The right claw is larger than the left.

The crab's soft body is twisted so that it can fit more easily into the spiral-shaped shells it lives in.

Hermit crabs have two eyes on the ends of stalks. These can move in all directions.

Hairy hermit crabs can live for 20 years, but they face terrible danger as they search for food or move to a new shell...

Arctic tern

The Arctic tern is an amazing long-distance traveller. It breeds in the Arctic, then spends 90 days flying 35,000 kilometres south to the Antarctic. It eats sea creatures including crabs and small fish.

1 When he mates, the male tern offers a gift of fish to his chosen female. The pair will stay together for life, making a nest in the same place on the ground each year.

2 Females lay two eggs and both parents take turns to keep them warm. The male carries on feeding his partner.

4 Once the chicks can fly, the colony of around 50 birds flies off to spend the summer in the Antarctic. They will return to the Arctic the following year to breed.

3 The chicks hatch after 22 days and are covered in soft grey or brown feathers. The parents feed them for a month while they learn to fly and hunt for themselves.

Did you know?

Arctic terns have sharp red beaks that they use to catch prey and to fight off attacks from other animals.

They have webbed feet like ducks, but they do not swim well and spend as little time as possible in the water where they feed.

The eggs are cream in colour with brown blotches so they are camouflaged with the pebbles around the nest.

Arctic terns can live for more than 30 years. Chicks and eggs are often at risk because the nests are on the ground...

Arctic fox

Arctic foxes eat mainly small animals called lemmings, but near the coast they will seek out bird eggs and chicks. Their thick fur is white in the winter and brown in the summer to blend in with the changing landscape.

1 Arctic foxes mate for life, producing a litter of cubs between May and June. The female makes a den for them, or takes over one dug by another animal.

2 The cubs suckle their mother's milk for 2—4 weeks but are soon weaned to eat meat. Out of a litter of 6—12 cubs only a couple will survive to become adults.

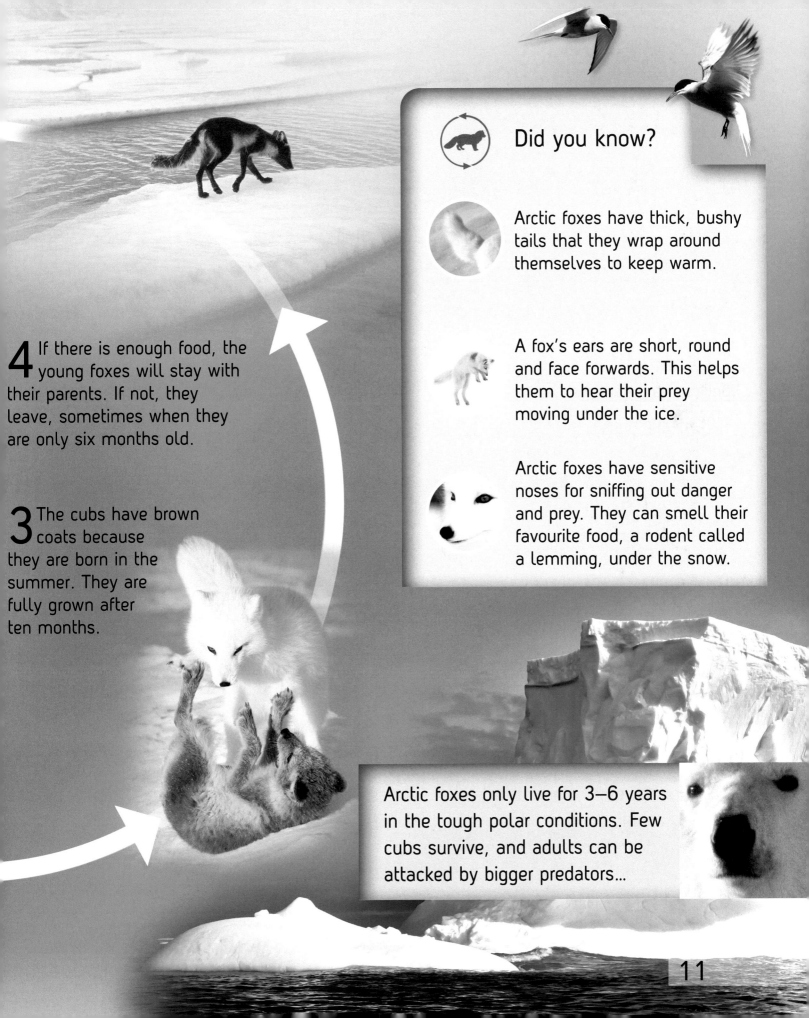

Arctic foxes have thick, bushy tails that they wrap around themselves to keep warm.

A fox's ears are short, round and face forwards. This helps them to hear their prey moving under the ice.

Arctic foxes have sensitive noses for sniffing out danger and prey. They can smell their favourite food, a rodent called a lemming, under the snow.

4 If there is enough food, the young foxes will stay with their parents. If not, they leave, sometimes when they are only six months old.

3 The cubs have brown coats because they are born in the summer. They are fully grown after ten months.

Arctic foxes only live for 3–6 years in the tough polar conditions. Few cubs survive, and adults can be attacked by bigger predators...

Polar bear

Polar bears are the kings of the Arctic. They eat mainly seals, but will attack and eat almost anything, including the Arctic foxes that often follow them, hoping to snap up their leftover food.

1 A pregnant female polar bear eats huge amounts of food to build up her strength for giving birth and feeding her cubs. She digs a large den in a snowdrift.

2 She gives birth to two helpless cubs that are blind for the first month of life and have hardly any fur. They rely on their mother's rich milk for food.

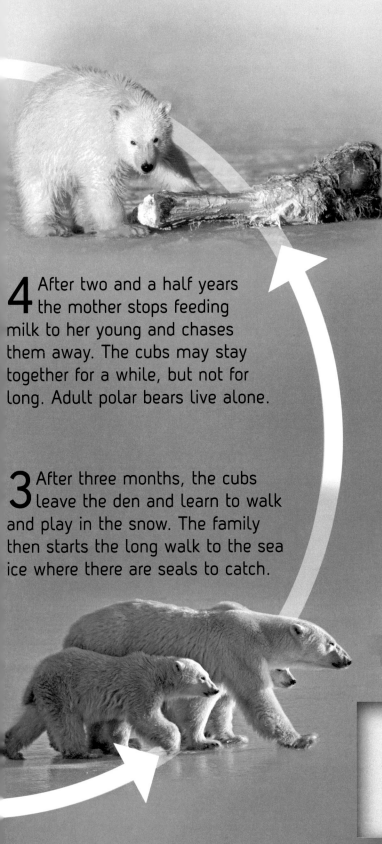

4 After two and a half years the mother stops feeding milk to her young and chases them away. The cubs may stay together for a while, but not for long. Adult polar bears live alone.

3 After three months, the cubs leave the den and learn to walk and play in the snow. The family then starts the long walk to the sea ice where there are seals to catch.

Did you know?

A polar bear's paws have thickly furred soles, making them non-slip on ice. Its claws are short and curved.

Polar bears have long, sharp teeth with gaps between for grabbing and holding prey. They swallow their food in large chunks.

Polar bears swim very well and spend as much time in the water as they do on land.

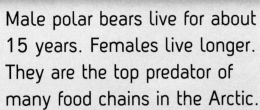

Male polar bears live for about 15 years. Females live longer. They are the top predator of many food chains in the Arctic.

Krill

Millions of small, pink shrimp-like krill float and swim together in huge swarms in all the seas, including the Antarctic ocean. Sometimes there are so many of them that the water looks pink.

1 The female produces thousands of eggs and the male fertilizes them. The eggs are then released into the water where they sink to the bottom and hatch into larvae.

2 As the larvae grow, they become too big for their hard exoskeletons, and they shed them. This happens every 8–15 days, 12 times altogether.

4 Adult krill feed at night. They eat tiny plants called phytoplankton that grow under the ice. By day, the krill sink down in the water as deep as 100 metres.

3 At first the larvae are fed by the yolk sacs in their bodies, but later they develop mouths and start to feed themselves.

Did you know?

Krill use their front six pairs of legs like brushes to collect food as they drift through the water. This is called filter feeding.

They have five sets of legs for swimming, called swimmerets, and others for cleaning themselves.

Krill can make blue-green light in their bodies. It may help them to find each other or to signal that a predator is nearby.

Krill live for 5–10 years but they are gobbled up in huge numbers by lots of animals, some as big as whales, others far smaller...

Antarctic silverfish

The waters around the Antarctic are cold enough to freeze most fish. The Antarctic silverfish has found a way to survive in icy waters and feast on the krill that live there.

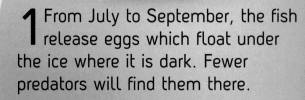

1 From July to September, the fish release eggs which float under the ice where it is dark. Fewer predators will find them there.

2 From November onwards, the eggs hatch into larvae. Each one is fed by a bag of food, called a yolk sac, attached to its body.

4 Adult silverfish try to hide from predators. Their silvery scales reflect the water around them like mirrors and this makes them more difficult to see.

3 Young silverfish breathe through their skin until their gills have formed. In this way, small pieces of ice cannot enter and damage their young bodies.

Did you know?

Silverfish have very large eyes so that they can see in water that is hardly reached by sunlight.

Their bones are very light, which helps them to stay afloat. They do not have a bag of gas inside their bodies to help them, as other fish do.

Adult silverfish have a chemical in their bodies that stops their blood freezing, even when the sea is as cold as −2° Celsius.

Antarctic silverfish can live for about ten years in waters where other fish would die. One bird loves to eat them, however...

Penguin

Adelie penguins are amazingly tough. They battle through harsh Antarctic storms to make an incredible journey: across the ice from the rocky land where they breed to the sea where they feed on fish and krill.

1 As summer begins in October, a pair of penguins makes a nest of stones on rocky land. The female lays two eggs and keeps them warm while her partner goes off to feed. He can be away for a week.

2 Seven weeks later, the first chick starts to peck its way through the egg's thick shell. It can take three days to break out. The chick calls to its parents so they will know its voice.

Did you know?

Penguins' smooth bodies make them great swimmers. They can zoom below the waves at up to 20 kilometres per hour.

Penguins can move fast on ice. They lie flat on their stomachs, push with their feet and steer with their flippers.

Their feet have claws that grip the ice, allowing them to waddle along at about four kilometres per hour.

4 Winter arrives in March and the adults and their young walk to the sea. They will return to breed after a round trip of about 13,000 kilometres.

3 When the chicks are eight weeks old, their parents leave them to go searching for food. The chicks huddle together for warmth. They start to grow waterproof feathers.

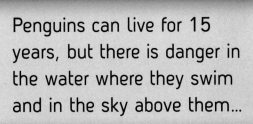
Penguins can live for 15 years, but there is danger in the water where they swim and in the sky above them...

Skua

The South Polar skua is not large, but it is a big bully. It flies to the Antarctic to breed, often nesting near Adelie penguins. It will raid the penguin colony for eggs and chicks to eat.

1 Skuas mate for life. A pair of birds scrapes out a simple nest on the ground or on a cliff. The female usually lays two eggs and both parents help to keep them warm.

2 The first chick is born after about four weeks. If food is in short supply, it will chase away the second chick that hatches out to make sure that it will have enough to eat.

Did you know?

A skua uses its short, curved beak for pecking rivals and ripping into food.

Its feet are webbed, with sharp claws. If threatened, a skua flies at its attacker with its claws stretched out in front of it.

Skuas have very long wings that can measure 160 centimetres from tip to tip. This helps them to fly long distances over the sea.

4 Adult skuas return to breed in the same place each year. They steal fish, eggs and chicks from penguins and other nesting birds.

3 At five weeks old, the chicks are still being fed by their parents. By eight weeks old, they will be ready to fly. They will get their darker, adult feathers after a few years.

The skua is such a fierce fighter that other animals usually try to keep out of its way. It has no predators.

Herring

Atlantic herring swim fast in huge groups called schools. They are always on the move between the coastal areas where they breed and the deep waters where they feed, including the seas around the Arctic.

1 Females lay at least 20,000 eggs, which sink and form a thick carpet on the seabed close to the shore. A lot of sea animals feed on these eggs.

2 After seven days, the eggs hatch into larvae. They have black eyes but the rest of their bodies are see-through and almost invisible in the water. They have no fins or scales.

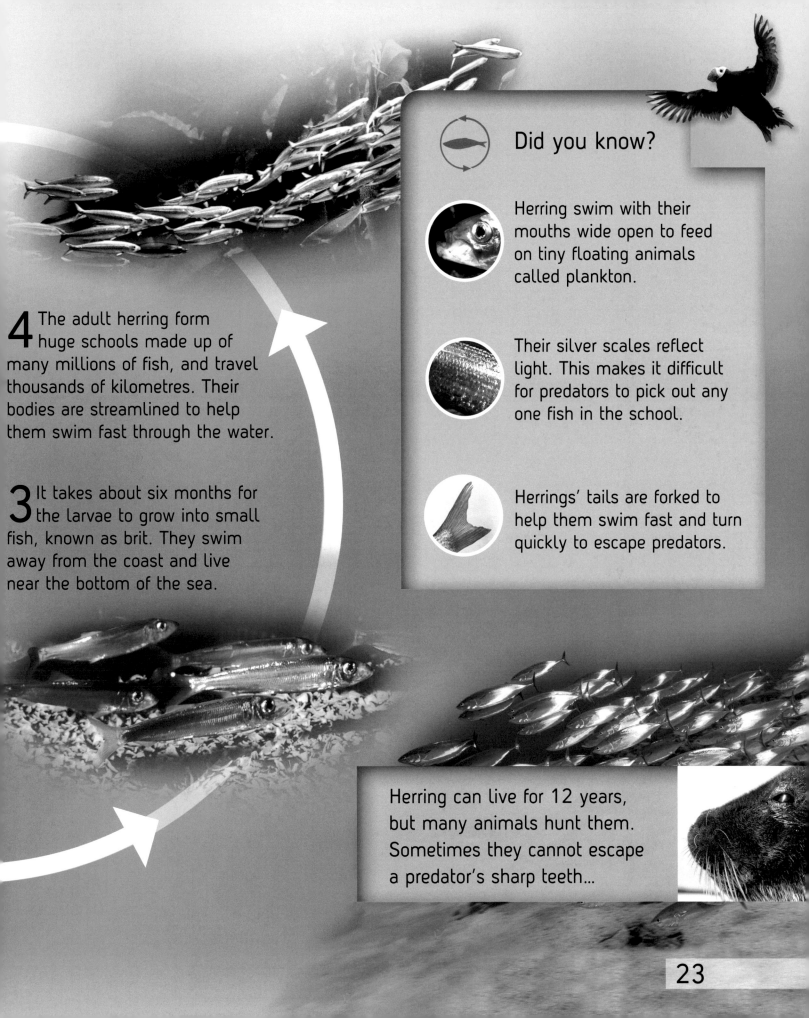

Did you know?

Herring swim with their mouths wide open to feed on tiny floating animals called plankton.

Their silver scales reflect light. This makes it difficult for predators to pick out any one fish in the school.

Herrings' tails are forked to help them swim fast and turn quickly to escape predators.

4 The adult herring form huge schools made up of many millions of fish, and travel thousands of kilometres. Their bodies are streamlined to help them swim fast through the water.

3 It takes about six months for the larvae to grow into small fish, known as brit. They swim away from the coast and live near the bottom of the sea.

Herring can live for 12 years, but many animals hunt them. Sometimes they cannot escape a predator's sharp teeth...

Seal

Ringed seals are fat and clumsy on ice and on land, but elegant when they swim in the water. They can dive to a depth of 45 metres to chase and catch fish, such as herring and cod.

1 When she has mated, the female builds a cave, called a lair, in the snow. There is a hole in the ice under it so she can dive into the water to hunt. She eats a lot so that she will have plenty of milk for her baby.

2 After nine months, a single pup is born. It suckles milk for about four weeks, doubling in weight and growing a thick layer of fat. It will shed its white fur after a month.

Ringed seals get their name from the pattern of black rings on their skin.

The back flippers are for swimming. The front ones have claws for scraping out holes and lairs in the ice.

Their small, earless heads and plump bodies are perfect for swimming. They can stay underwater for 45 minutes.

4 Adults spend most of their time in the water, but they come onto the ice once a year when they shed their skin. Females can breed from the age of four, but males have to be older.

3 As soon as the pup is weaned off milk, the mother leaves and it must look after itself. It lives on its blubber, or fat, while it learns to hunt.

Ringed seals live for about 20 years. The biggest threat is from polar bears, but another white, furry animal will attack too...

Arctic wolf

Wolves roam large areas of the Arctic. They can attack animals bigger than themselves because they hunt in packs. They eat musk oxen and reindeer as well as smaller prey, such as seals.

1 Wolves mate for life. They find a den where the female will give birth. This could be a cave or a den left by another animal. Both parents raise their young.

2 Nine weeks after mating, the female gives birth to about six pups. They are blind and deaf so they rely on the pack for food and protection. Their mother stays with them in the den.

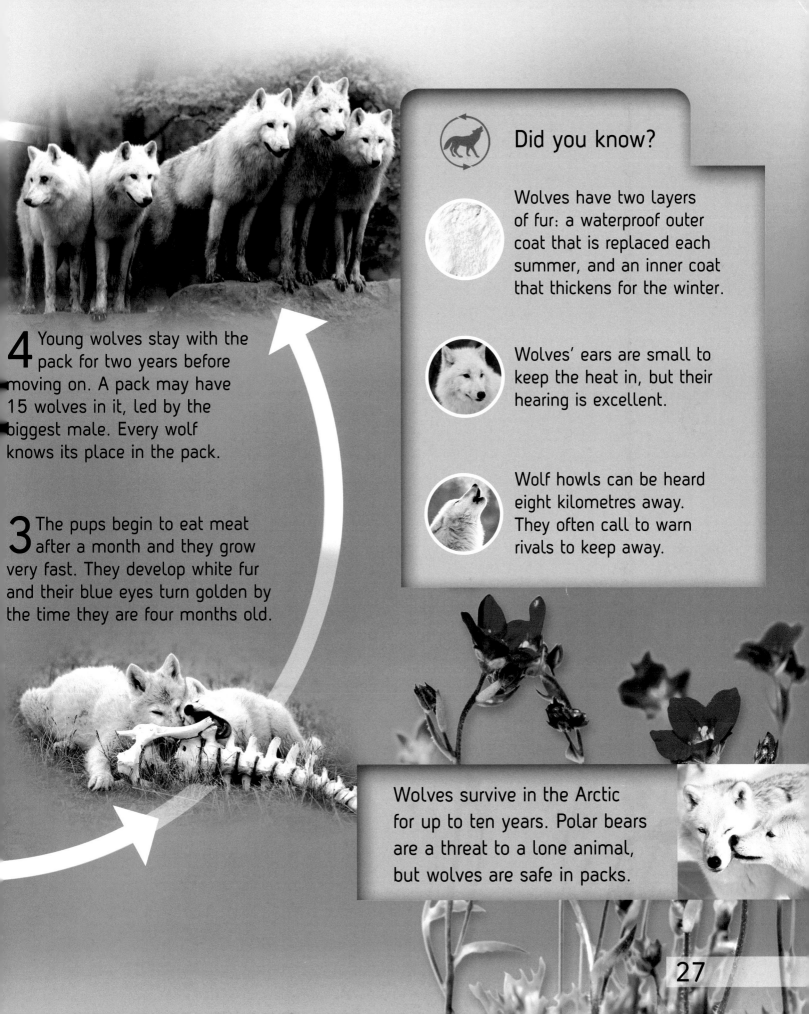

4 Young wolves stay with the pack for two years before moving on. A pack may have 15 wolves in it, led by the biggest male. Every wolf knows its place in the pack.

3 The pups begin to eat meat after a month and they grow very fast. They develop white fur and their blue eyes turn golden by the time they are four months old.

Did you know?

Wolves have two layers of fur: a waterproof outer coat that is replaced each summer, and an inner coat that thickens for the winter.

Wolves' ears are small to keep the heat in, but their hearing is excellent.

Wolf howls can be heard eight kilometres away. They often call to warn rivals to keep away.

Wolves survive in the Arctic for up to ten years. Polar bears are a threat to a lone animal, but wolves are safe in packs.

An Arctic food web

This book follows some polar food chains. Most animals eat more than one food, however, so they are part of many food chains. There are lots of food chains in the polar lands, and they link up like a map to make a food web.

Polar bear

Arctic wolf

Orca

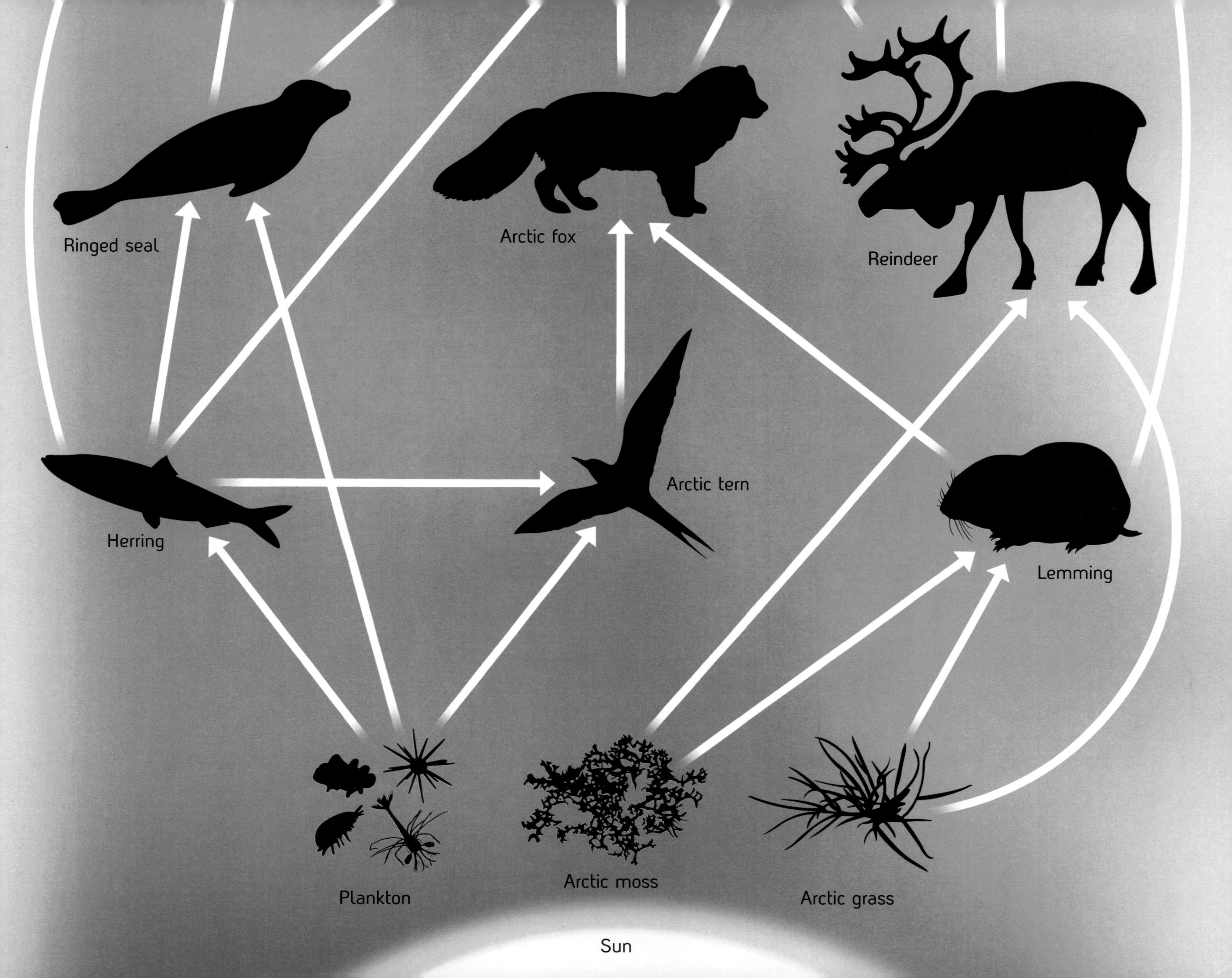

Reindeer

Lemming

Arctic grass

Arctic moss

Sun

Arctic fox

Arctic tern

Plankton

Ringed seal

Herring

Glossary

ALGAE
Plant-like living things that make their food using the sun's energy.

CAMOUFLAGE
Blending in with the surroundings to avoid being easily seen.

COLONY
A group of the same kind of animals that live together.

CONSUMER
An animal that survives by eating other living things.

DEN
A wild animal's home.

EXOSKELETON
A hard shell on the outside of an animal's body.

FERTILIZE
When sperm from a male animal joins with the egg of a female to make a new life.

FLIPPERS
The flat, wide limbs belonging to a swimming animal.

GILLS
The organs used to breathe underwater.

HABITAT
The natural home of an animal.

LARVA
A young animal that will change its body shape to become an adult. Groups are called larvae.

LICHEN
This living thing is a partnership between a fungus and an algae. It makes its own food.

MATE
When a male and female animal reproduce.

NUTRIENT
Anything that a living thing takes in to give it energy and to help it grow.

OMNIVORE
An animal that eats plants and other animals.

PACK
A group of the same animal that live and/or hunt together.

PLANKTON
Tiny living things that drift in seas and oceans. If they are plants, they are called phytoplankton.

PREDATOR
An animal that kills and eats other animals.

PREY
An animal hunted by a predator.

PRODUCER
A living thing that makes its own food from the energy of the sun.

RIVAL
Two animals are rivals when they both want the same thing.

SAC
A bag of food attached to a baby animal.

SCALES
The small, hard, flat plates on the surface of a fish's skin.

SCAVENGER
An animal that eats dead animals or plants.

SCHOOL
A large group of fish that swim together.

SEA ICE
Frozen ocean water.

SHED
When an animal gets rid of the outside of its body. This is also called moulting.

STALKS
The long, thin body parts that hold up another body part (see the hairy hermit crab, pages 6–7).

SUCKLE
When a young animal drinks milk from its mother's body.

WEAN
When a baby stops drinking milk from its mother and eats solid food instead.

WEBBED
When the toes are joined together with thin skin.

YOLK
The goodness inside an egg that feeds a new baby animal.

These websites have information about the polar lands, or their animals, or both!

- 42explore.com/polar.htm
- bbc.co.uk/nature/places/arctic
- enchantedlearning.com/school/Antarctica
- a-z-animals.com/reference/polar-regions
- kidsbiology.com/biology_basics/biomes/what_are_biomes_1.php
- www.natgeokids.com/uk/animals/
- hubpages.com/animals/polarbearaware-2

Index